Charlie
and
the Queen's hat

La collection Hello Kids READERS fait suite à l'album illustré *Hello, I am Charlie from London*. Ces lectures en anglais sur 4 niveaux nous entraînent dans d'extraordinaires aventures pleines de suspense avec Charlie, un jeune Londonien et ses copains.

Chaque niveau est déterminé par le nombre de *headwords* contenu dans chaque livre. Ce mot anglais est l'équivalent d'une entrée, comme dans un dictionnaire, pour laquelle un groupe de mots partage le même sens : les mots *look, looks, looking* correspondent ainsi à une seule entrée et constituent un seul *headword*. Le titre *Charlie and the Queen's hat* totalise 138 *headwords*.

Chaque titre de la collection propose :
- des textes illustrés en couleurs,
- une double-page lexique en images,
- une double-page d'informations culturelles,
- un CD audio avec les enregistrements du récit et du lexique.

Pour faciliter la compréhension de l'histoire et l'acquisition du vocabulaire, les mots importants sont marqués d'un astérisque.

Avec la participation de :
Mme Patricia Decol-Baron, *conseillère pédagogique Langues Vivantes, académie de Versailles.*

www.abcmelody.com

Charlie

and
the Queen's hat

written by Sue Finnie & Danièle Bourdais
illustrated by Yannick Robert
narrated by Lauren Monchar

This is Charlie.

Charlie: Hello! My name's Charlie.
            I'm 9 years old.
            I like football.
            I like my friends… and my cat*.
            And I love cupcakes*!

Charlie is at school. His teacher* is Miss Todd.

Miss Todd:	Good morning, children*.
Class:	Good morning, Miss Todd.
Shana:	Excuse me, Miss Todd...
Miss Todd:	Come in, Shana!

Miss Todd:	Thank you, Shana.
Charlie:	What's in the envelope, Miss?
Miss Todd:	It's an invitation.
	Oh! What a surprise!
Charlie:	I like surprises!

Stella:	Is it an invitation to a party?
Miss Todd:	Yes, Stella.
	It's an invitation for all the class...
	to the Queen*'s garden* party.
Charlie:	The Queen's garden party?
	Is it at Buckingham Palace?
Miss Todd:	Yes, Charlie, it is!
Charlie:	Wow!

Charlie: When is the party, Miss?
Miss Todd: It's on Saturday.
Charlie: Do we wear our school uniform?
Miss Todd: No, no school uniform on
              Saturday, children!
              Wear really smart clothes.

It's Saturday. Charlie is in his bedroom*.

Dad: Wear the blue shirt*, Charlie.
Charlie: I don't like the blue shirt, Dad!
               I prefer the white shirt.
Mum: Yes, the white shirt is smart.

Dad:	I like the green jacket* and the blue tie*.
Charlie:	Is this OK, Mum?
Mum:	Very smart! But not the yellow socks*, Charlie!!!

A big red bus is waiting at the school.

Charlie: Hi, Stella.
Stella: Hello, Charlie.
Charlie: I like your red dress*.
             It's very pretty.
Stella: Thank you! Your jacket is smart
             too, and I like your tie!

It's time to go.

Charlie: Look at Abdul!
Stella: I love the bow tie*, Abdul.
Abdul: Thank you! Harvey has a bow tie too!

The children are on the bus.

Charlie: Look at the flags*.
Stella: Wow! It's very beautiful!
Abdul: I can see Buckingham Palace.

Stella:	Buckingham Palace is BIG.
Charlie:	I like the guards*.
	Their uniform is smart.
Abdul:	Yes, and their hats are funny!

Abdul:	I've got my camera*.
	Let's take a photo!
Charlie:	OK. Look, I'm a guard too!
Stella	Oh, Charlie! Ha ha ha!

In the Palace garden…

Charlie:	It's a beautiful garden.
Stella:	Listen. What's that?
Abdul:	Music! There's a band*.
Charlie:	Great band! I love it!

It's the big moment: the Queen arrives.
The band plays the National Anthem.

Charlie:	Look, it's the Queen!
Abdul:	She's very smart!
Stella:	Ooh... It's very windy!
	I don't like the wind.

The wind blows away the Queen's hat*.

The Queen:	Welcome… Oh no! My hat!
Abdul:	Stupid wind!
Charlie:	The Queen is sad.
	Let's find her hat!

Stella:	Look, over there!
	The hat is in the tree.
Charlie:	Yes, maybe. Be careful, Stella!
Stella:	I'm OK.

But it's not the Queen's hat, it's a bird*!

Stella: Oh no! Look at my dress!
            It's ruined.
Charlie: Poor Stella!

Abdul:	Look, over there!
	Is that the Queen's hat in the lake*?
Charlie:	Yes, maybe.
Abdul:	Pass me a branch...
Charlie:	Be careful, Abdul!
Abdul:	I'm OK.

But it's not the Queen's hat, it's a plastic bag*.

Abdul: Ahhhh! Oh no! Look at my shirt!
                And my bow tie! I'm soaking wet!
Charlie: Poor Abdul! Poor Harvey!

Charlie sees a horse* near a tree. He's got an idea.

Abdul: Be careful, Charlie!
Charlie: I'm OK.
Stella: Can you see the Queen's hat?

Charlie:	No, I can't see the Queen's haaa... hat!
Stella:	Oh Charlie... be careful!
Abdul:	Ha ha ha !
Charlie:	Oh ! Look at my jacket... and my shirt... and... Wait a minute!

Stella: What is it, Charlie?
Charlie: Look! Over there!
                Is that the Queen's hat
                behind the bush*?
Abdul: Yes, Charlie, it IS the Queen's hat!

Miss Todd:	Charlie, Stella, Abdul!
	Look at you!
Charlie:	Your Majesty, here's your hat!
The Queen:	Thank you very much.
	This is my favourite hat.

The Queen:	What's your name?
Charlie:	Charlie, Your Majesty.
	I'm really sorry. We're very dirty.
The Queen:	You are a bit dirty…
	but you are heroes!
	Come and have tea* with me.

It's time for tea.

The Queen:	Have some tea!
Stella:	A sandwich for me, please.
Charlie:	A cupcake, please.
	I love cupcakes.
Abdul:	Harvey likes cupcakes too!
All:	Ha ha ha!

Royal Britain

The Royal Family lives in Buckingham Palace in London. The palace has a big garden.

The Royal Family likes garden parties and invites lots of people.

The Royal Family has a castle at Windsor, near London, and a big house at Sandringham.

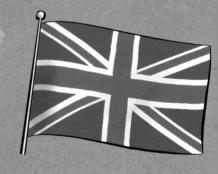

The British flag is called the Union Jack. It is red, white and blue.

There are royal palaces in Scotland too, at Holyrood and Balmoral.

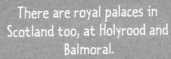

The Royal Guard at Buckingham Palace anges every day at 11.30am. If you see four guards, the King or Queen is there. If you see two guards, he or she is not at home.

The British National Anthem is called *God save the Queen*, when there is a Queen, and *God save the King*, when there is a King.

band

bedroom

bird

bow-tie

bush

camera

cat

children

cupcake

dress

flag

garden

guard

hat

horse

jacket

lake

plastic bag

queen

shirt

socks

tea

teacher

tie

Hello Kids READERS — Charlie and the Queen's hat
D'après *Hello, I am Charlie from London* de Stéphane Husar
ISBN 978-2-36836-034-7 / © 2014 ABC MELODY Éditions, Paris, France
www.abcmelody.com
Loi n°49-956 du 16 juillet 1949 sur les publications destinées à la jeunesse.
Dépôt légal : octobre 2014 - Imprimé en Turquie
Direction artistique : Stéphane Husar - Coordination collection : Lucie Tournebize
Maquette : Valentin Gall